MODERN WARFARE

Air Warfare

By Martin J. Dougherty

Please visit our Web site www.garethstevens.com. For a free color catalog of all our high-quality books, call toll free 1-800-542-2595 or fax 1-877-542-2596.

Library of Congress Cataloging-in-Publication Data

Dougherty, Martin J.
      Air warfare / by Martin J. Dougherty.
            p. cm. _ (Modern warfare)
      Includes bibliographical references and index.
      ISBN-10: 1-4339-2720-9   ISBN-13: 978-1-4339-2720-1 (lib. bdg.)
      1. Air warfare_Juvenile literature. 2. United States. Air Force_Juvenile literature. I. Title.
UG631.D68   2010
358.4_dc22   2009019086

This North American edition first published in 2010 by
Gareth Stevens Publishing
111 East 14th Street, Suite 349
New York, NY 10003

Copyright © 2010 by Amber Books, Ltd.
Produced by Amber Books Ltd., Bradley's Close
74–77 White Lion Street
London N1 9PF, U.K.

Amber Project Editor: James Bennett
Amber Copy Editors: Melanie Gray, Jim Mezzanotte
Amber Designer: Andrew Easton
Amber Picture Research: Terry Forshaw, Natascha Spargo

Gareth Stevens Executive Managing Editor: Lisa M. Herrington
Gareth Stevens Editor: Joann Jovinelly
Gareth Stevens Senior Designer: Keith Plechaty

Interior Images
Cody Images: 17
Edwards Air Force Base: 15
Eurofighter: 10
Military Visualizations, Inc.: 1, 6, 11, 22, 25
Northrop Grumman: 14
Tyson V. Rininger: 12
U.S. Department of Defense: 3 (U.S. Air Force), 4, 5, 7, 8 (U.S. Air Force), 9 (U.S. Air Force), 13, 16 (U.S. Air Force), 18 (U.S. Air Force), 19, 20 (U.S. Air Force), 21 (U.S. Air Force), 23 (U.S. Air Force), 24 (U.S. Navy), 26 (U.S. Air Force), 27 (U.S. Air Force), 28 (both), 29

Cover Images
Front cover: U.S. Department of Defense

Printed in the United States of America

CPSIA Compliance Information: Batch #CR011090GS: For further information contact Gareth Stevens, New York, New York at 1-800-542-2595

▶ **STEALTH TAKEOFF**
A B-2 Spirit stealth bomber takes off from an air base in Nevada.

CONTENTS

CHAPTER 1

FIGHTING FROM THE AIR

There are many ways to win a battle. One way is to get help from the sky. Since World War II (1939–1945), aircraft have played a big part in warfare. They help armies and navies defeat enemies.

Aircraft help in many ways. They hit targets on land and at sea. They also patrol the skies so that enemy planes cannot attack. Some aircraft spy on enemies. Others move troops and supplies.

▶ STRIKE EAGLE
The F-15E Strike Eagle, invented by the United States in the 1980s, can carry many different weapons. It can use **missiles**, bombs, or guns to attack targets on the ground. It can also fight other planes in the air.

Countries use different kinds of aircraft to fight battles. They use small, fast fighter planes and large bombers. They also use helicopters.

▲ ABOVE THE CLOUDS
This Russian Tu-95 "Bear" can fly very long distances. It is a bomber that can attack targets far from its base.

A New Way to Fight

When World War I (1914–1918) began, planes had not been around long. At first, they acted as scouts. They watched enemy troops on the ground. A few planes dropped bombs. Later, fighter planes began to take part in air battles called "dogfights."

By World War II, planes were more powerful. Fighter planes were fast.

DID YOU KNOW?

At first, pilots shot at each other with handguns. They even threw bricks from their open cockpits! Later, machine guns were installed on the fronts of planes. Those aircraft became the first fighter planes.

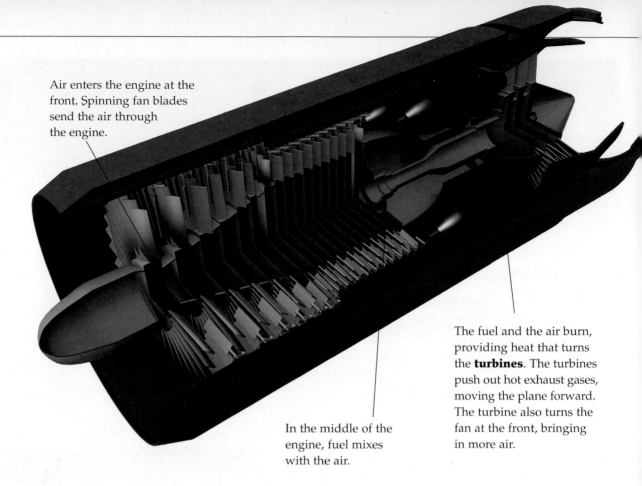

Air enters the engine at the front, Spinning fan blades send the air through the engine.

The fuel and the air burn, providing heat that turns the **turbines**. The turbines push out hot exhaust gases, moving the plane forward. The turbine also turns the fan at the front, bringing in more air.

In the middle of the engine, fuel mixes with the air.

▲ A JET ENGINE

Most fighters and bombers use jet engines. Those engines are lightweight but powerful. They work well at a high **altitude**. Jet planes can travel very fast over long distances.

DID YOU KNOW?

Sound travels at about 768 miles (1,236 kilometers) per hour. We call the speed of sound Mach 1. Many fighter planes travel faster than the speed of sound. Some aircraft travel at Mach 2. Each increase in Mach number equals an increase in speed.

Planes fought each other, and they hit targets on land. They began flying from **aircraft carriers**, ships that provide planes with a place to land at sea. Soon, larger, more advanced planes dropped bombs. Enemy troops tried to shoot the planes down, but the aircraft escaped quickly.

The Jet Age

During World War II, most planes had propellers in front. The propellers "pulled" the planes through the air. The planes used

piston engines. Cars and trucks also use that kind of engine.

After the war, planes began using jet engines (*left*). Those engines push a plane forward. They suck in air at the front. The air mixes with fuel, and that mixture burns. Exhaust gases rush out the back.

Jet engines enable planes to fly fast. Today, some fighter planes fly more than 20 times as fast as a car!

Hide and Seek

Pilots use bombs and missiles to hit targets that are far away. Missiles are rockets that find targets on their own. Some missiles use **radar**. A missile sends out radio waves. The

▼ LOADING MISSILES
Only one or two people fly fighter planes, but it takes a team to load the missiles and **ammunition** into the plane. This team is loading a missile into a U.S. F/A-18 Hornet fighter.

waves bounce off a target and return to the missile. Then the missile knows where to go.

During battles, pilots try to hit targets, but they must also keep from getting hit! Pilots and ground troops use radar and missiles to detect and shoot down enemy planes.

Becoming a Pilot

An air force has many people. Only a few people fly planes. Most people have other jobs. They fix planes, or they make sure the planes have supplies, including fuel.

▲ IN TRAINING
Pilots learn to fly in special planes, called trainers, before they fly fighter jets. Instead of jet engines, most trainers have propellers. Trainers do not need to fly as fast as fighter jets.

IN THEIR OWN WORDS

*"Every fighter pilot must pass a **g-force** screening, riding in a **centrifuge**, before ever touching an actual fighter aircraft."*

U.S. Air Force Capt. Jammie Jamieson, F-22 pilot

Fighter pilots need a lot of training. First, they go to college. Then they take many tests. If they do well, they go on to flight school. To serve in the U.S. Air Force, fighter pilots attend flight school for more than a year.

▼ LEARNING TO FLY
U.S. Air Force Gen. Don Cook (*left*) tries out the C-130J Hercules aircraft simulator. The simulator enables him to make mistakes and try again, just like in a computer game.

CHAPTER 2

FIGHTER AND ATTACK JETS

Small military planes usually do specific jobs. Most fighter jets battle other planes to control the skies. Attack jets hit targets on land and at sea. Some fighter jets can patrol the skies *and* hit targets.

Attack planes fight air battles to keep enemies away. They hit enemy planes trying to attack their planes, ships, and ground troops. Fighter planes also hit ground targets to help their troops win battles. They target tanks with **artillery**, or big guns. They also hit enemy supplies.

Up Close and Far Away

Sometimes, fighter jets battle enemy planes at close range. They shoot powerful guns called **cannons**. Those guns fire thousands of bullets per minute. Pilots must fly

▼ EUROFIGHTER
Engineers from several countries in Europe designed the Eurofighter Typhoon in the 1980s and 1990s. Those same countries now use the Typhoon in their military forces. It can fly at more than 1,300 miles (2,000 km) per hour. The Typhoon can also drop bombs and fire missiles.

skillfully. They must turn, climb, and dive quickly. If they do not, they may get hit!

Fighter pilots also attack planes from a distance. The pilots might not even see the enemy aircraft. Instead, pilots use radar to find enemy planes. Then the pilots fire missiles that are guided by radar or that are designed to follow the heat released from the enemy's jet engines.

Attack jets often come in just before land battles begin. First, they strike enemy weapons. Then attack planes hit troops or artillery. They drop bombs and fire missiles.

▼ **A-10 THUNDERBOLT II**
The U.S. A-10 Thunderbolt II, designed in the 1970s, is very tough. Its job is to attack targets on the ground. The Thunderbolt II, nicknamed "Warthog," can fly even when it is badly damaged.

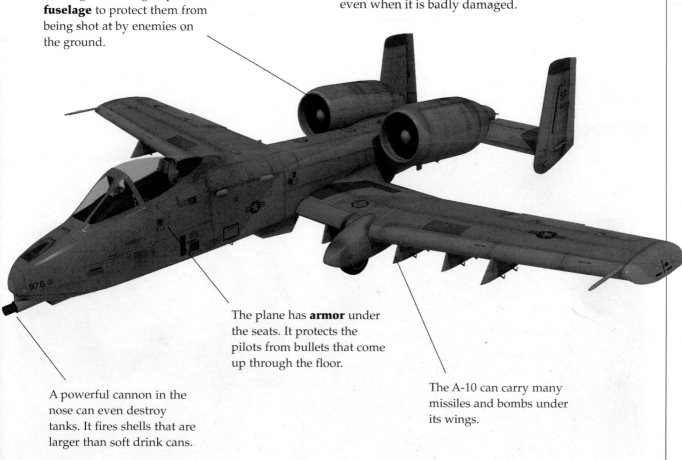

The engines are high up on the **fuselage** to protect them from being shot at by enemies on the ground.

The plane has **armor** under the seats. It protects the pilots from bullets that come up through the floor.

A powerful cannon in the nose can even destroy tanks. It fires shells that are larger than soft drink cans.

The A-10 can carry many missiles and bombs under its wings.

Attack jets can hit small targets that are hard to reach. They might be near **civilians** who are not fighting. Sometimes targets are close to troops. Pilots fly in low and fast. When they are close to their target, they launch a direct hit.

Fooling the Enemy

Sometimes attack pilots can trick enemy missiles by dropping hot flares. Missiles designed to look for heat go after those flares. Attack pilots can also shoot metal pieces called **chaff**. Missiles guided by radar go after the chaff.

Attack pilots also fly in **stealth** planes. Those planes have a special shape and paint job to make them harder to see on radar. Radar does not bounce back from

DID YOU KNOW?
The F-22 Raptor can fly in ways that are almost undetectable. On enemy radar screens, it appears to be the same size as a ½-inch (12 millimeter) steel ball bearing!

▼ AFTERBURNERS
The engines on this F-22 Raptor use **afterburners** for extra power. The engines burn extra fuel in the exhaust gas. Jets with afterburners use a lot of fuel, but they are very fast.

them, so machines that pick up radar signals do not detect them. Hot exhaust from their engines is cooled before it is released, making it harder for heat-seeking missiles to strike them.

High-Tech

The F-22 Raptor is a U.S. fighter jet, but other countries use it, too. It can attack ground targets, but its main job is fighting air battles. It is a stealth fighter.

The Raptor has powerful computers. They help the pilot fly and hit targets at the same time. Other planes need two people to do those tasks. Inside the cockpit, many computer screens display information to help the pilot.

Pilots cannot look down when they are busy. The Raptor has a heads-up display, or HUD. That is a see-through screen. It shows information right in front of the pilots.

▲ **F-22 RAPTOR**

The F-22 Raptor is one of the fastest fighter jets ever built. It can turn quickly to dodge an enemy. It carries missiles and guns to shoot down other aircraft. Its top speed is secret.

IN THEIR OWN WORDS

"*[The F-22] is a magnificent machine, but it's a completely different generation of aircraft. It gives you a wealth of information, [which] I have to absorb and then quickly process.*"

Royal Air Force Flight Lt. Dan Robinson, the first British pilot to fly the F-22 Raptor

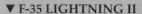

▼ F-35 LIGHTNING II
The newly designed F-35 can fly faster than the speed of sound and then land like a helicopter with a vertical drop. Because this stealth fighter plane is hard to see with radar, it is difficult to shoot down.

A Plane for the Future

The newest U.S. fighter jet is the F-35 Lightning II, which is still being tested. The United States plans to begin using that fighter jet in 2011. Other countries will use it, too.

Three different fighter jets will be built. One will use runways on land. Another will take off from and land on aircraft carriers. A third will take off from very short runways and land like a helicopter!

▼ HIGH-TECH HELMET

Pilots of the F-35 Lightning II use a special helmet to help them fly the plane. This helmet is a test version. The one that pilots will use in combat will be smaller.

The helmet projects information in front of the pilot's eyes. It shows the aircraft's speed and indicates exactly where to aim guns and missiles.

The helmet can tell the direction in which the pilot is looking. The pilot can aim his or her weapons without removing his or her hands from the controls.

CHAPTER 3

BOMBERS

Like attack jets, bombers can help during battles. But they have even more advantages. Bombers can fly longer than other jets without needing more fuel. Bombers can also fly deep into enemy territory without being detected. They can hit targets that many attack jets cannot reach.

Bomber planes are larger than attack jets, so they have more space for weapons. Bombers can carry many missiles and bombs, including powerful **nuclear** bombs.

IN THEIR OWN WORDS

"There are four crew members on the B-1B, and we all have our own separate jobs to do, but we have to work together, to make [a strike] happen."

U.S. Air Force Lt. Col. Frank Swan,
B-1B weapon systems officer

▼ B-1B LANCER
The U.S. Air Force has used the B-1B since the 1980s. It is a very fast bomber that can attack distant targets. It is also hard to spot on radar.

Supersonic

Some bombers fly very fast. They are **supersonic** bombers. They can fly faster than the speed of sound. One such plane is the U.S. B-1B Lancer. It can hit targets and get away quickly.

The Tu-160 Blackjack is a Russian supersonic bomber. It looks a lot like the B-1B, but it is larger and faster. It can fly at almost twice the speed of sound.

Both of those planes have "swept" wings to help them fly faster. After takeoff, the wings sweep in close to the plane's body. A bird's wings work the same way.

DID YOU KNOW?

The B-52 is a U.S. bomber that was invented in the 1950s. It is not supersonic. But it has done many important jobs, such as serving U.S. pilots in the Vietnam War (1957–1975), the Cold War (1940s–1990s), and the Persian Gulf War of 1991.

▼ TU-160 BLACKJACK
This Russian supersonic bomber can travel long distances and carry regular bombs as well as long-range nuclear weapons.

▼ **B-52 STRATOFORTRESS**
The powerful B-52 has been used since the 1950s. It has eight jet engines, but it is not very fast. B-52s can launch missiles or drop bombs.

"Smart" Weapons

In the past, bombs were simple. They could not find targets on their own. When bombs were dropped, they did not always hit their intended targets.

Today, some bombs are "smart." They use Global Positioning System (GPS) technology. Smart bombs get signals from satellites in space. Those signals tell smart bombs exactly where to strike.

Other bombs are guided by crew members. They aim a beam of light called a **laser**. The bombs follow the laser. Crew members guide missiles, too. They "steer" them into position with a **joystick**. The missiles have cameras, so crew members can watch where they go.

Stealth Bomber

The B-2 Spirit is a U.S. plane that has been in use since 1997. It is a stealth bomber that is hard to see or detect. It sneaks up on enemy targets. The enemy never knows it is there.

The B-2 looks like a boomerang. The whole plane is a wing. When it flies, there

18

is a lot of **lift**. Lift is the force of air pushing from under the wings that enables planes to fly.

When the B-2 is in the sky, radar is fooled. Radar detectors show a tiny speck, the size of an ant. It's almost invisible. The B-2's engines are deep inside its body, so the plane stays quiet and cool. Heat-seeking missiles cannot detect it.

Bombers in Action

Stealth bombers have helped U.S. troops in Afghanistan. In that country, enemy bases are hidden in mountains. Ground troops have trouble reaching those bases, but bombers can strike them easily. The planes fly very high, away from enemy attacks, and drop smart bombs. Those bombs go right to their targets, no matter how small.

DID YOU KNOW?
Global Positioning System (GPS) technology was invented for the U.S. military. Today, people use GPS in their cars to guide them to unfamiliar places. GPS tracking via cell phones can also help search-and-rescue teams find people who are lost or in danger.

▼ B-2 SPIRIT
The B-2 is not as fast as a B-1B and does not carry as many bombs as a B-52, but it is hard to detect. It can fly quickly to any place in the world, bomb its target, and return home without being spotted by the enemy.

CHAPTER 4

SUPPORT AIRCRAFT

Some planes do not fight, but they still help win battles. To do so, they keep watch. Those planes are reconnaissance planes. They find out what enemies are doing. Pilots of reconnaissance planes search for information by flying into enemy territory and recording information.

Reconnaissance planes are often similar to fighter jets. Instead of weapons, they carry special gear. They take pictures from a great distance. They "listen" to what the enemy is saying. Watching enemies can be dangerous. Pilots have to be careful. Enemies might try to shoot them down!

Planes Without Pilots

Reconnaissance planes do not always have pilots. Some are Unmanned Aerial Vehicles, or UAVs. Remote operators control those planes from far away. The planes have

▼ REMOTE-CONTROLLED PLANE
This MQ-9 Reaper UAV carries missiles to attack enemy targets. It is controlled by an operator who is safe on the ground, hundreds of miles away.

cameras, so the operators know where the planes are going.

Remote-controlled planes fly to dangerous places. If enemies shoot them down, no one gets hurt. Operators use those planes to "see" around hills or far away. Operators also use the planes to fire missiles and drop bombs.

Filling Up

Some planes provide fuel to jets while they are in flight. Planes use a lot of fuel. They usually have to land to get more. Flying tankers deliver the fuel to keep them going.

Refueling in midair is tricky. The tanker plane has a long pipe or hose that trails behind it. The plane needing fuel must fly close and connect to it. Both planes must stay in position while fuel is transferred from the tanker plane to the other.

▲ **MIDAIR REFUELING**
Refueling in midair from a flying tanker is difficult. Pilots have to practice. Refueling in the air enables pilots to fly longer patrols at greater distances from their bases.

DID YOU KNOW?

The MQ-9 Reaper is the latest U.S. Unmanned Aerial Vehicle (UAV). It was designed in 2001 to carry missiles and bombs. Crews take it apart and pack it up. Then the plane's parts travel on a regular plane. Halfway around the world, other crews put the Reaper back together so it is ready to fly!

Early Warning

Pilots use radar to search for enemies, but it can find only those who are nearby. To help locate distant enemies, pilots get help from special planes.

Those aircraft have a powerful radar system called Airborne Early Warning and Control (AEW&C). That system is very powerful. The planes can find enemies from far away. They tell fighter and bomber pilots what enemies are doing. Then the pilots know how to attack.

▼ AIRBORNE EARLY WARNING
Airborne Early Warning and Control planes do not carry weapons, but they do an important job. Powerful radar searches for enemy aircraft and activities. This E-3 Sentry is used by many countries, including the United States and France.

The E-3 carries radar equipment in this pod. The radar can scan the sky for hundreds of miles and track many aircraft at once.

Without radar, the E-3 is not much different from a regular airliner. Instead of passenger seats, it has huge computers.

The E-3 needs four powerful engines to fly with all of its equipment. The plane stays in the air for hours at a time.

Transport Planes

When armies need to get around quickly, they call on transport planes to do the job. Transport planes help move troops and equipment. They can go to places that ships or trucks cannot reach.

Transport planes are often big. Many countries use the Il-76. It is a Russian plane. That huge plane carries heavy loads. The U.S. C-17 Globemaster III is also a large plane. It can land on dirt runways. Both planes have big doors in back that flip down for easy loading.

▲ **HEAVY TRANSPORT**
A C-17 Globemaster III can land almost anywhere—including on a dirt runway. It can carry many loads, such as troops, supplies, mail, and even tanks.

IN THEIR OWN WORDS

"My jet was loaded with cargo, and I landed between two bomb craters on a 3,500-foot [1,067-meter] section of runway. My landing distance was 3,380-feet [1,030 m]!"

U.S. Air Force Capt. Justin Riddle,
C-17 Globemaster III pilot, on flying into Afghanistan

CHAPTER 5

HELICOPTERS

Helicopters are slower than planes, but they can fly in small spaces where planes cannot. Helicopters do not need runways. They can hover in place in the air. They can fly very slowly, too. They can also fly sideways or backward.

A helicopter has long blades called rotors that are like wings. They spin around, lifting the helicopter. The small rotor at the back of the helicopter helps it point in the right direction. If a rotor gets damaged, the helicopter will crash. Different helicopters do specific jobs.

▼ SHIP-TO-SHIP TRANSPORTATION
It is very difficult to move people and supplies between ships in the middle of the sea. This MH-60S Knighthawk helicopter is delivering supplies to a U.S. Navy aircraft carrier.

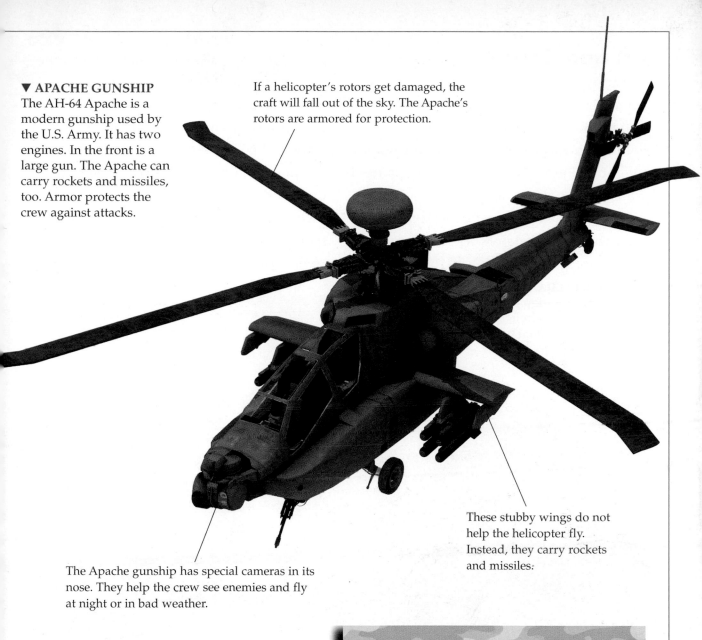

▼ APACHE GUNSHIP
The AH-64 Apache is a modern gunship used by the U.S. Army. It has two engines. In the front is a large gun. The Apache can carry rockets and missiles, too. Armor protects the crew against attacks.

If a helicopter's rotors get damaged, the craft will fall out of the sky. The Apache's rotors are armored for protection.

These stubby wings do not help the helicopter fly. Instead, they carry rockets and missiles.

The Apache gunship has special cameras in its nose. They help the crew see enemies and fly at night or in bad weather.

Gunships

Some helicopters attack targets on the ground. Those attack helicopters are called gunships. They are equipped with guns and missiles. Gunships can hide from enemy forces. They are often used to hunt and destroy tanks. Gunships may hover behind a hill or some trees for cover. Then they quickly pop out and **ambush**, or surprise, the enemy.

DID YOU KNOW?
The Russian Mi-12 was the biggest helicopter ever built. It was designed in the 1960s to carry missiles and space rockets. It could lift more than 40 tons (36 metric tons).

Lift and Carry

Helicopters often carry troops and supplies. They can quickly reach places that trucks and planes cannot. The helicopters swoop in and drop off troops for battle. Later, they bring the troops food, water, and ammunition.

Transport helicopters are massive. They can carry many soldiers. They can even carry artillery or small vehicles. Each pilot lets out a long cable. The cable gets attached to a load. Then the helicopter lifts it into the air. That kind of job takes skill!

The UH-60 Blackhawk is a U.S. helicopter, but many other countries also use it. It was designed in the 1960s and has two engines. Two engines are safer than one and give more power for heavy lifting. There are

▼ GUNSHIP PILOT
This Apache gunship pilot has a special helmet to help him fly. The lens in front of his eye is a computer screen that shows him important information.

▲ AFGHANISTAN MISSION
An Mi-8 helicopter is about to fly a reconnaissance mission in Afghanistan. Its mission is find the enemy. Then ground forces or planes can attack.

different Blackhawks for different jobs. The U.S. Navy, Army, Air Force, and Marine Corps all use those helicopters for different tasks. They can carry heavy loads and can fire weapons. Blackhawks can also remove injured soldiers from dangerous battles and take them to military hospitals or safe zones.

Search and Rescue

Blackhawk helicopters also go on search-and-rescue missions. Helicopters are perfect for those operations since they can hover in place. Helicopters can also move easily in cramped spaces that are hard to reach.

DID YOU KNOW?
Like some fighter pilots, Apache crew members wear special helmets. The helmets are attached to the Apache's guns. When the crew members turn their heads, the guns turn, too.

If they cannot land, crew members can rescue a person with a cable. They lower the cable to bring the person to safety.

Aircraft carriers have search-and-rescue helicopters. The helicopters rescue pilots who have crashed in the sea. They also rescue civilians on sinking ships. Search-and-rescue missions are dangerous. Helicopters often go out during bad storms.

▲ NIGHT FIRING
This MH-53 helicopter is firing its weapons at night. The sky looks green because the picture was taken with a special camera that can see in the dark.

▼ HELICOPTER REFUELING
Tanker planes can refuel helicopters, but it is a hard job. The tanker must fly very slowly. This helicopter is a U.S. Marines CH-53 Super Stallion. It is refueling off the coast of Africa.

Helicopters in Action

In 1991, Apache gunships were helpful in the Persian Gulf War. That war was fought in the desert. Because the gunships had no hills to hide behind, they flew at night. The gunships flew very low to the ground to surprise the enemy. They hit many tanks.

Helicopters have also helped troops in Afghanistan. Those craft are easy targets for enemy attacks, but they are useful. Helicopters can bring troops into mountains. They can fire missiles and get away quickly.

▲ APACHE IN IRAQ
An AH-64 Apache helicopter gunship flies over Iraq. In 1991, gunships helped ground forces defeat Iraqi forces by destroying Iraqi tanks and other vehicles.

Helicopters are different from fighter planes and bombers, but all those aircraft have one thing in common: They all help win battles. They travel fast and far, and they hit targets that are hard to reach. Without them, many battles would be lost!

GLOSSARY

afterburners—devices in jet engines that burn extra fuel in the hot exhaust to give the engines more power

aircraft carriers—a military ship with a flight deck on which fighter and attack planes can be launched and landed

altitude—an aircraft's height above ground, measured as the distance from sea level

ambush—a surprise attack made from a hidden place

ammunition—the objects that guns fire, such as bullets and shells

armor—a protective covering placed on vehicles as a defense against weapons

artillery—huge guns used by land forces that can fire shells great distances

cannons—large, powerful guns on airplanes that can fire many bullets

centrifuge—a device that spins a person around at high speed and helps pilots learn how they will feel when flying fast jet planes

chaff—tiny pieces of metal scattered by aircraft to confuse radar

civilians—people who are not in the military and who are not fighting in a war

fuselage—the main body of a plane

g-force—the force of gravity or acceleration felt by a person or an object

joystick—a lever that a pilot pushes in different directions to control a plane

laser—a powerful beam of light

lift—the force of flowing air beneath an airplane's wings that keeps the aircraft up

missiles—rockets that fly to a target and explode

nuclear—a type of energy created by splitting atoms of certain chemical elements; nuclear bombs use this energy to create huge explosions

piston—the part of an internal combustion engine in which the fuel burns; burning fuel makes pistons move up and down, which creates the spinning motion that turns the wheels or propeller

radar—a system that uses radio waves to detect aircraft or other objects; radar sends out radio waves that bounce off the object and are then detected by a receiver

rotors—the winglike blades on a helicopter that spin around to create lift

simulator—a device that lets people pretend to do something, such as flying; for pilots learning to fly, simulators have all the controls of a real plane

stealth—a type of technology that enables an aircraft or another vehicle to avoid being detected by enemy troops or radar

supersonic—faster than the speed of sound

turbines—spinning wheels with fan blades used in jet engines; turbines push out exhaust gases to move the plane forward

FOR MORE INFORMATION

Books

The AH-64 Apache Helicopter. Cross Section (series). Ole Steen Hansen (Capstone Press, 2005)

Air War. Crabtree Contact (series). Antony Loveless (Crabtree Publishing, 2008)

Air Warfare of the Future. Library of Future Weaponry (series). Randy Littlejohn (Rosen Publishing, 2006)

B-2 Stealth Bombers. Torque: Military Machines (series). Jack David (Children's Press, 2007)

Fighter Planes. Up Close (series). Andra Serlin Abramson (Sterling, 2008)

U.S. Air Force Spy Planes. Blazers (series). Carrie A. Braulick (Capstone Press, 2006)

Web Sites

F-22 Raptor
www.lockheedmartin.com/products/f22
Examine photos of the F-22 Raptor, and watch a video that shows the plane in flight.

How Stuff Works: Stealth Bombers
www.science.howstuffworks.com/ stealth-bomber.htm
Read details about the invention of the B-2 bomber, learn more about its technology, and see a video of it in flight.

Nova: Faster than Sound
www.pbs.org/wgbh/nova/barrier
Discover more about supersonic aircraft, including the first planes to break the sound barrier. Find out why a supersonic plane makes a sonic boom.

U.S. Air Force
www.airforce.com/learn-about
Learn more about the U.S. Air Force and its history. Enter a "hangar" to discover different aircraft.

INDEX

ABOUT THE AUTHOR

Martin J. Dougherty holds a Bachelor of Education degree from the University of Sunderland in the United Kingdom. He has taught throughout northeast England and his published work includes books on subjects as diverse as space exploration, martial arts, and military hardware. He is an expert on missile systems and low-intensity warfare.